Copycat First Courses Recipes

55 Tasty First Courses, Quick and Easy to Prepare at Home Even if You are not a Gourmet Chef

ISBN: 978-1-80182-084-4

Table of Contents

3

RICE, ANCHOVIES, FENNEL, BOTTARGA

Servings: 4 persons

Cooking Time   Cost   Difficulty

Ingredients:

- 360 gr of rice
- 60 gr of fresh fennel
- 100 ml of soy milk
- 1 lemon
- 150 gr of fresh anchovies
- 1 fennel
- 120 lt of sunflower seed oil
- 120 gr of mullet roe
- 1.5 lt of water
- 10 gr of anchovy casting

Directions:

Wash and clean fresh anchovies by removing the head and bones. Wash and chop the fresh fennel and add it to 60 g of seed oil.

Wash the lemon and grate the peel to obtain the zests.

Marinate the anchovies for 40 minutes in the oil with the fennel and lemon zests.

Prepare the soy mayonnaise by adding the milk in a carafe and whipping with the remaining seed oil with electric whips as in a classic mayonnaise. Store in the refrigerator.

Boil the water in a saucepan. Cut the fennel in brownise. Put a handful of coarse salt in a pan. Add the rice and toast it until warm to the touch. Cook for 11 minutes adding hot water when the risotto dries, without ever overcooking.

Stir in soy mayonnaise, browned fennel and anchovy dripping. Leave to rest with lid for 2 minutes.

Return the rice to the heat, add a ladleful of boiling water and bring back to the boil, then turn off again.

Grate the mullet roe at the base of the dish with a microplane. Drain the anchovies marinated in oil and lay them on top of the roe, then add the rice and finish with a drop of oil.

GRILLED CHEESE AND PEPPER

Servings: 1 person

Cooking Time	Cost	Difficulty

Ingredients:

100 gr Spaghetti

Pepper

30 gr Pecorino

5 gr Pecorino cheese

20 gr Parmesan Cheese 30 months

Directions:

Cook the spaghetti in plenty of boiling salted water for 8 minutes, leave them in water at 60° for 5 minutes then dip them in cold water to stop cooking. Grill them again with the hat technique to intensify colors and scents for 6 minutes; put them on a small one to make sure they do not fall out.

Combine the grated pecorino and Parmigiano cheese and eat them with a little spaghetti cooking water.

Mix 7 types of pepper including: Nepal timut pepper, Sichuan black pepper from China, Sarawak black pepper from Malaysia, white pepper from Indonesia, long pepper from Himalaya, green pepper from Vietnam, wild pepper from Madagascar. Manteca spaghetti with cream cheese, sprinkle with grated pit pecorino cheese and pepper.

WHITE, YELLOW AND RED PASTA

Servings: 4 persons

Cooking Time   Cost   Difficulty

Ingredients:

- 240 gr buffalo stracciatella cheese
- mint and basil
- 240 gr paste giant propellers
- e.v.o. oil
- 100 gr yellow tomatoes
- salt
- 100 gr cherry tomatoes
- pepper

Directions:

Cook the pasta in plenty of salted water. Dissolve the stracciatella of buffalo. Pass the yellow tomatoes in a non-stick pan with a drizzle of extra virgin olive oil: you will need to heat them taking care not to let them unpack. Divide the tomatoes into 4 slices and dress them with a little oil, salt and pepper. Drain the pasta al dente and pour a drizzle of extra virgin olive oil. Lightly sauté the propellers in the pan scenting them with basil and mint leaves.

Decorate the base of each base dish with the buffalo rag and cover with the propellers. Garnish the composition with notes of color, alternating yellow and red tomatoes.

TAGLIATELLE WITH ARTICHOKES AND SCAMPI

Servings: 4 persons

Cooking Time   Cost   Difficulty

Ingredients:

- 270 gr flour 0
- 8 scampi
- 30 gr grated grana padano cheese
- 30 gr semolina
- 280 gr egg noodles
- extra virgin olive oil
- 11 yolks
- 3 artichokes
- 5 lemon juice
- butter
- clove of garlic
- Salt and pepper

Directions:

Prepare the dough, put the flours on a marble surface, add the egg yolks and a tablespoon of oil, mix well. Work the dough for a long time as it softens. At this point, start pulling it into very thin sheets from which to make the tagliatelle.

Clean the artichokes well by shortening them and cutting the thorny part, divide them into quarters by removing any beard inside, then cut them again in half. Put on the fire a pan with a little oil and the clove of garlic, just hint at

sauté the artichokes, add salt and pepper, then add the lemon juice immediately so that the artichokes remain clear; continue cooking until the artichokes are cooked but not unmade. Remove the head from the scampi and cut them in half with a very sharp knife, season the fleshy part with salt and pepper and cook them for a few minutes in a small non-stick pan with a little oil, first on the fleshy part then on the carapace. Keep warm for a few moments until serving. Put on the fire a pot with plenty of salted water and as soon as it boils, throw the pasta that will cook in a few minutes; drain it directly into the pan where the artichokes were cooked by adding 30 g of butter flakes and stir.

RICE WITH CANTALOUPE MELON AND BEATEN CAPERS

Servings: 4 persons

Cooking Time   Cost   Difficulty

Ingredients:

- 320 gr rice
- Parsley
- 1 cantaloupe melon
- bread croutons
- 50 desalinated capers
- 1 tablespoon white wine vinegar
- white wine
- 80 gr extra virgin olive oil
- Salt
- Pepper

Directions:

Wash the melon well, remove the seeds and skin and prepare a broth with these scraps by boiling them in water for 30 minutes. Chop the capers and dress them with oil, vinegar and parsley. Cut the melon pulp into cubes and keep it aside. Toast the rice in a saucepan, wet with white wine and cook for 14 minutes slowly adding the melon stock.

5 minutes before cooking, add the diced melon and, when cooked, stir in oil. In a serving dish pour the risotto and sprinkle with chopped parsley capers and decorate with some small bread croutons.

BEET DUMPLINGS AND POTATO FOAM

Servings: 4 persons

Cooking Time   Cost   Difficulty

Ingredients:

- 1 fresh beets mint and basil
- Salt
- 125 gr corn-starch
- 1 lemon
- pepper
- 200 gr potatoes
- black truffle to taste
- 30 gr smoked ricotta
- 1 knob of butter

Directions:

Remove the leaves from the beets, cook them with the skin for about 30 minutes in boiling water. Drain them, peel them, blend them and place the purée obtained in a cloth. Let it drain in a sieve for one night so that it loses all its water. To taste, perfume with mint and basil, which then have to be eliminated. The next day tie the past with corn-starch. Form the dumplings with the help of two spoons and cook them in boiling water for 30 seconds/1 minute. Prepare the mashed potato with the boiled potatoes, oil, salt, a few drops of lemon juice and pour it into a siphon.

ROULADE WITH BROCCOLI, TOMATO AND COD

Servings: 4 persons

Cooking Time   Cost   Difficulty

Ingredients:

- 200 gr red wine pasta
- 5 gr white pepper   4 gr thyme
- 27 gr gelatine powder
- 100 gr broccoli
- 34 gr basil
- 250 gr coppered tomatoes
- 150 gr clams
- 4 gr marjoram
- 50 gr cod fillets
- extra virgin olive oil
- 30 gr smoked ricotta
- lemon and orange peel

Directions:

Wash and prick the cod, then cover it with whole sea salt, orange and lemon peel; place it in a vacuum and let it rest for three hours. Take the cod out of the vacuum, wash it and cut it into 4 mm cubes. Blanch the tomatoes, then cool them, peel them and remove the skin and seeds. Chop everything finely with a knife, then season with oil, salt, pepper, thyme. Bring the tomato to 40 ° C, add the gelatine powder. Cool. Set aside a few tablespoons of tomato and mix the rest with the cod cubes. Cut the tops of the broccoli so that they are slightly larger than the ravioli and more or less the same size. Peel the pasta to 1.2 mm thick, cut to 58 mm long and 49 mm wide. Pack the ravioli by placing a small ball of tomato between two thin layers of pasta. Take the ravioli for the longest part and wrap them around a broccoletto on each side. Dip the clams in boiling water flavoured to taste for about 40 seconds. Drain and place in water and ice. Shell. Cook the pasta in acidulous salted water. Dissolve in a pan the tomato jelly set aside with a drizzle of oil, add the clams, basil, a grated lemon zest and emulsify by turning the pan. Place the clam sauce on the serving plate and arrange the ravioli rolls. Sprinkle with smoked ricotta rape. Pasta with red wine.

RISOTTO WITH 'NDUJA AND BURRATA CREAM

Servings: 4 persons

Cooking Time   Cost   Difficulty

Ingredients:

- 300 gr of rice
- 200 gr of Burrata Cheese
- ½ glass of white wine
- beet sprouts
- 40 gr of 'nduja
- walnut kernels
- 60 gr of butter
- 100 gr of parmesan cheese

Directions:

Start the preparation of the risotto by toasting the rice dry in a casserole. When it is hot enough, and the grains cannot be held in your hand, blend with the white wine. Then proceed to cooking in the usual way, adding salted boiling water little by little. Cook for about 15 minutes. Turn off the heat and add the 'nduja, butter and grated Parmesan cheese. Stir vigorously, adding a ladle of hot water if necessary, to keep the risotto soft.

While the rice is cooking, pass the Burrata Cheese with all the cream to the immersion blender, whipping lightly. When serving, drop the risotto in large "drops" on the plate and repeat the operation with the burrata. Add the crumbled nuts and beet sprouts.

LEMON WATER SPAGHETTINI AND PROVOLONE CHEESE

Servings: 4 persons

Cooking Time   Cost   Difficulty

Ingredients:

- 4 untreated lemons
- Lemon leaf flour
- 700 ml of water
- Evo Oil
- 360 g of spaghetti
- Pepper and salt
- 130 g of Provolone

Directions:

Wash the lemon leaves thoroughly. Dry them and put them on a baking tray to dry at 60 degrees for 12 hours. Dust them with a mixer, then sieve the powder.

Cut out the lemon peels, already washed, with a potato peeler and put them to macerate in water overnight. Once ready, filter the water, removing the peels. Bring the lemon water to the boil in a pan wide enough to hold the dough. Add the spaghetti, a turn of oil and bring them to cooking, shaking them in the pan until they soften.

Only then you can begin to stir gently.

Spaghetti are a fragile format; you must be careful not to break them. When the dough is cooked, stir out of the fire with grated Provolone del Monaco, then finish the dish with pepper, oil and a sprinkling of lemon leaf flour.

PASTA WITH URCHINGS, SANAPO AND CUTTLEFISH

Servings: 4 persons

Cooking Time   Cost   Difficulty

Ingredients:

- Gnucchitti
- Pizzuliati
- Patrinisters
- 1 Cuttlefish
- Chilli pepper
- 2 Lemons
- 4 tablespoon urchins eggs
- Patrinisters
- Garlic
- 1 tapenade mocha teaspoon
- Raw sanapo leaves
- Oil
- Lapsang Souchong Smoked Tea

Directions:

Three different formats of handmade pasta are used for patience pasta: gnucchitti, pizzuliati and patrinostri.

Make a sauce of sanapo with vegetable broth, blanched leaves, potato, salt, oil, water, raw curls seasoned with lemon juice, evo oil, parsley, chili pepper. Cut the lemon into a diamond shape. Prepare the patience dough (if you have any, this is not for sale). Blanch the cuttlefish meat counting up to 5, drain it and pour it in a bowl where there is already cuttlefish cut into julienne; season it like curls. Take the tenderness of the raw sanapo leaves (chewing them you will have the memory of wasabi in your mouth) and keep them aside. In a pan, lightly fry the garlic, oil, chili pepper and 1 teaspoon of tapenade mocha, 2 fresh bay leaves, sea urchin water and Lapsang Souchong smoked tea.

Composition of the dish.

Drain the pasta, sauté it in a pan with a little smoked evo oil, place the sanapo sauce on the plate, place the patrons standing and fill them with raw curls. Add more curls here and there, decorate with curly cuttlefish, sprinkle with 5 lemon diamonds and complete the dish by placing the raw leaves of sanapo.

SHRIMP AND ZUCCHINI RICE

Servings: 4 persons

Cooking Time   Cost   Difficulty

Ingredients:

- 320 gr of rice
- Half a clove of garlic
- 500 gr of shrimp tails
- Half a glass of white wine
- 2 large zucchinis
- A tablespoon of chopped parsley
- Olive oil
- Salt

Ingredients: For shrimp soup:

- Half coast of celery
- The shrimp carapaces
- Half onion
- 1 kg of ice with one litre of water or 2 litres of cold water
- Half a clove of garlic
- Half cup of brandy
- 1 carrot
- Salt

Directions:

Clean the shrimp from the shells and cut the back with a small knife. Remove the intestines and rinse the shrimp under running water.

Place the shrimp carapaces well stretched out on a plate with a sheet of baking paper. Turn on the oven grill and toast the shrimp shells for 10/12 minutes, turning them over every now and then. In the meantime, prepare the broth by cutting the celery, carrot and onion into small pieces and brown the vegetables in a saucepan with a drizzle of olive oil and half a clove of crushed garlic. When the vegetables are withered add the shrimp carapaces toasted in the oven, stir for a few seconds, add a pinch of salt and pour water and ice. Adjust the heat to minimum and let it simmer for 30 minutes.

Blend with an immersion blender and filter the shrimp broth with a narrow mesh strainer.

Bring the broth to the boil and keep it warm.

Cut the zucchini into small cubes (as shown in the video recipe), brown them in a pan with a couple of tablespoons of oil and half a clove of crushed garlic and keep them aside.

In a saucepan, toast the rice, fade with white wine and when it has evaporated start adding, little by little, the boiling shrimp broth. Mix and cook like a normal risotto.

When the risotto is al dente add the diced zucchini, shrimps whole or cut in half (depending on size) and a pinch of chopped parsley. Stir until the shrimps are cooked, adjust the flavor with a pinch of salt and ground pepper, turn off the heat and maintains with a drizzle of olive oil.

Serve the shrimp and zucchini risotto decorating the dish with some whole shrimp and some parsley leaves.

FETTUCCINE WITH BLACK TRUFFLE

Servings: 4 persons

Cooking Time   Cost   Difficulty

Ingredients for Fettuccine

- 500 gr Semi-wholemeal flour
- 2 gr salt
- 280 gr Water
- 40 gr Natural Yeast

Directions:

Place the flour in a fountain on the work surface, pour the salt, water and yeast in the centre, then knead trying to mix well the ingredients and work vigorously, finally let the dough rest for 3 hours at 26-28 ° C. Roll out the fresh dough with a rolling pin, roll out the dough and cut strips about 2 cm wide and at least 12 cm long in order to obtain the fettuccine.

Ingredients:

- 1 White Onion
- Brandy
- 1 Vanilla Berry
- 1 Anchovy
- Laurel
- Butter
- Thyme
- parsley
- Sage

Directions:

Wilt the onion in butter with laurel, thyme and sage in a pan.

Add the black truffle coarsely grated with a pinch of vanilla (seed from the pod), and let it simmer for a few minutes.

Cook the fettuccine in boiling salted water, then drain them and sauté them in the black truffle sauce.

Pour them in the dishes and serve.

SMALL CANNELLONI OF TURBOT AND COD FISH

Servings: 8 persons

Cooking Time   Cost   Difficulty

Ingredients for pasta green

- 200 gr flour
- 35 gr cooked spinach
- 1 egg Water
- 1 albumen

Directions:

Knead the 4 mixtures separately, place the compounds under vacuum to rest for 24 hours. Then pull out strips of dough about 1/2 cm thick and stack them on top of each other until you reach 8 layers. At the end you will have a brick of layered dough of different colors. Cut a "slice" of about 1 cm and pass it to the dough puller transversely so as to obtain a puff pastry. Blanch it, cool it and let it dry giving it the typical cannelloni shape.

Ingredients for red pasta

- 250 gr flour
- 2 eggs
- 1 tablespoon of tomato paste
- Ingredients for yellow pasta
- 200 gr flour
- 2 eggs

Ingredients for Cuttlefish Black Pasta

- 200 gr flour
- 1 teaspoon of cuttlefish black
- 2 eggs

Ingredients for the filling:

- 1 large turbot of about 2 kg
- Thyme
- stale bread
- Marjoram
- 1 onion
- Basil
- 1 garlic
- Dry white wine
- extra virgin olive oil
- Salt and pepper

Directions:

Fillet and dilute the turbot. brown the onion, add garlic and thyme to taste, and then the meat of the turbot. Smoke with a little white wine, add a little stale bread, marjoram, basil to taste. regular salt and pepper. Pass everything to the meat grinder.

Ingredients for guazzetto:

- 1 redfish
- Celery
- 2 ripe tomatoes
- Carrots
- Chilli pepper Onions
- Cod Tripe

Directions:

Blanch the cod tripe and clean them. Prepare a base of celery carrots and onions, brown, add the redfish and turbot bones. Continue to brown, add tomatoes, water and ice to cover. boil for about 1 hour. Filter and reduce again by half. When it is well tasty, add the cod tripe and continue to cook for a few minutes, the gelatine contained in the tripe will serve as a thickener. Stuff the cannelloni with the turbot mixture, heat them with steam, then place them on the tripe.

PURPLE RICE WITH BEEF TARTARE

Servings: 4 persons

Cooking Time   Cost   Difficulty

Ingredients:

- 200 gr rice
- 60 gr ox hip tip
- 1 glass of white wine
- hazelnut grain
- 1 red cabbage
- extra virgin olive oil
- 1 blonde onion
- Butter
- Grana cheese
- 100 gr of lard
- 50 gr cream
- Salt and pepper

Directions:

Clean the onion, chop it and brown it in a pan with butter. Add the rice and toast it until it takes a nice blond color. Smoke with

34

white wine and, once evaporated, wet the rice with water where the red cabbage has been previously stewed. Cook the rice for about 20 minutes, stirring constantly and keeping it covered with water.

Cut the lard into small pieces and melt it in the cream. Season with salt and pepper.

Beat the meat with a knife and season with a drizzle of oil and hazelnut grains. Once the rice is cooked, stir in butter and parmesan cheese.

Place the risotto and finish it, decorating with the seasoned tartare, lard sauce and dill leaves.

MALTAGLIATI WITH CALF AND ARTICHOKES

Servings: 4 persons

Cooking Time   Cost   Difficulty

Ingredients:

- 140 gr flour "00"
- 240 gr calf sweetbread
- 100 gr durum wheat semolina
- 40 gr celery
- 2 eggs
- 40 gr carrots
- 6 artichokes
- 40 gr onions
- 80 gr white wine
- 40 gr flour
- 80 gr brown bottom
- extra virgin olive oil
- Parsley
- Salt and pepper

Directions:

In a pastry board, mix the two types of flour and mix them with the eggs and a pinch of salt. Knead vigorously and leave to rest for 15 minutes. Roll out a thin sheet of dough and cut into small rectangles.

Clean the artichokes, cut them into julienne and cook over high heat with a little oil. Wash the sweetbreads carefully and cook them in plenty of lightly salted water with the chopped vegetables. Drain them, remove the skin and shell them in small bites. Season with salt, pepper, lightly flour them, sauté them in a little butter and then add the artichokes. Wet them with white wine and beef stock, allowing them to reduce. Cook the maltagliati in plenty of salted water, drain them and add them to the mixture. Mantecare with grated Parmesan cheese and chopped parsley. Serve immediately.

RICE WITH PUMPKIN RISOTTO, LICORICE

Servings: 4 persons

Cooking Time   Cost   Difficulty

Ingredients:

- 1 kg pumpkin violin
- 3 carrots
- 700 gr rice   2
- coasts of celery
- 80 ml extra virgin olive oil
- 3 vegetable broth
- 3 glasses of dealcolized white wine
- licorice in block
- 100 gr cold butter cut into cubes
- 3 shallots
- 250 gr parmesan cheese
- nutmeg

Directions:

Clean, wash and chop the shallot, celery and carrot very finely. In a saucepan with 50 ml of oil fry this chopped mixture; as soon as it is golden brown, add the pumpkin.

diced and let it flavor for about 15-20 minutes. Wet with the broth and cook for another 20 minutes, then go to the mixer and sieve.

In a casserole suitable for rice, toast the rice with 30 ml of extra virgin olive oil, when the rice is warm to the touch add three glasses of white wine, dealcolized, and then three ladles of broth.

Add the pumpkin seasoning and proceed to cooking by adding one ladle of broth at a time and stirring continuously.

When after about 18-20 minutes the rice will have finished cooking, remove it from the heat and mix it with cold butter, Parmesan cheese and nutmeg. Serve in a holster and sprinkle with freshly grated licorice.

EGG ... WITH CAVIAR

Servings: 4 persons

Cooking Time   Cost   Difficulty

Ingredients:

- 4 Big Eggs
- Chives
- 10 gr Caviar
- Hazelnut oil
- 16 Durum wheat semolina shells
- White pepper
- 40 gr Water
- Salt

Directions:

Blanch the shells in lightly salted water for 2 minutes and cool them immediately in water and ice. Beat the yolks and egg whites vigorously, remove the foam and leave to rest for at least 30 minutes. Repeat the operation 3 times, then add the water and adjust the salt and white pepper. Pour the mixture thus obtained into the pasta and steam at 85°C for 10 minutes. Arrange 4 shells for each diner. Season with hazelnut oil, finely chopped chives and caviar.

SCALLOPS FETTUCINE

Servings: 4 persons

Cooking Time   Cost   Difficulty

Ingredients:

- 16 scallops
- basil
- 100 gr cherry tomato
- 1 garlic
- 2 spring onions
- oil
- 1 dl thick fish stock
- Salt

Directions:

Crush the scallops between two sheets of baking paper until a thin sheet is obtained and put in the refrigerator. In a frying pan fry in oil the garlic clove, the tomatoes cut in half, the spring onion cut in julienne, salt and brown. Add the fish stock and cook for a few minutes. Recover the scallop sheet, cut them into strips like strips, put them in the steam oven for 5 seconds and then add them to the sauce, adding a few basil leaves. Spaddle and serve hot garnishing with fried and crunchy onion.

RICE WITH BRITTANY OYSTERS

Servings: 4 persons

Cooking Time   Cost   Difficulty

Ingredients:

- 20 gr chopped chives
- 16 oysters
- 80 gr onions blanched and cut into cubes
- 250 gr rice
- burrata weighing at least 100 g
- 20 gr butter
- 30 gr herring eggs
- 1 l vegetable broth
- glass of white wine
- 1 dl extra virgin olive oil

44

Directions:

Shell the oysters being very careful not to break the shellfish and to keep the water inside the shell. In a large saucepan toast the rice for a few moments. Smoke with the white wine and continue cooking, wetting periodically with a little fish stock and stirring continuously. 5' before the desired cooking, wet with the filtered oyster water. Let it dry for 2-3' at most. Remove from the heat, add the shelled oysters, 10 g of chopped chives, butter, oil and maintains with a wooden spoon vigorously so as to obtain a creamy risotto. Spread the risotto on 4 hot plates. Place 7-8 pieces of burrata cheese, oysters, onion, herring caviar and the rest of the chives on top of each plate. Season with 1 drizzle of oil and serve immediately.

CHICKPEA SOUP WITH MULLET AND TRUFFLE

Servings: 4 persons

Cooking Time   Cost   Difficulty

Ingredients:

- 250 gr dry chickpeas
- 1 garlic
- 4 mullets
- rosemary
- 60 gr black truffle
- extra virgin olive oil
- 200 gr broken linguine
- Salt and pepper

Directions:

Soak the chickpeas in mineral water overnight and cook them in plenty of water.

46

Scale, gut and fillet the mullets, brown the carcasses with oil, garlic and rosemary and wet with 2 ladles of water. Boil for about 5 minutes, then pass everything through a fine sieve keeping the stock aside.

In a pot grate the truffle, brown for 30 seconds, add the mullet stock, then the chickpeas and their cooking water. Bring to the boil and add the pasta. After 2 minutes complete with the fillets of mullet cut into cubes. Remove from the heat when the pasta is still very al dente.

FUSILLI WITH RED SHRIMP, LICORICE AND BOTTARGA

Servings: 4 persons

Cooking Time   Cost   Difficulty

Ingredients:

- 320 gr fusilli
- some gills of mullet bottarga
- 16 shrimps
- shrimp bisque
- 500 gr turnip tops
- 30 gr onion
- 50 gr butter
- 50 gr white wine
- Salt
- licorice powder

Directions:

Shell the shrimps and deprive them of the central gut, cut them into chunks and set aside.

For the bisque brown the heads and what remains of the shell of the shrimp with butter, a little onion and black pepper, wet with wine and let it evaporate. Cover with water and cook for 45 minutes, strain, reduce and adjust salt.

For the turnip tops cream blanch in plenty of salted water, drain and let cool in water and ice. Set aside a few thumbtacks for the garnish and lightly sauté the rest with a little garlic and onion. Wet with water and cook for about 20 minutes, then blend everything together.

Brown the shrimp with a drizzle of oil, salt them slightly, wet with bisque and add the turnip tops. Cook the pasta in boiling salted water, drain a few minutes before cooking time and finish cooking in a pan with the shrimp and turnip tops.

AMBERJACK TIMBALE

Servings: 4 persons

Cooking Time   Cost   Difficulty

Ingredients:

- 600 gr amberjack fillet slice
- soy sauce
- 2 zucchinis
- breadcrumbs
- 200 gr basmati rice
- Salt and pepper
- extra virgin olive oil

Directions:

Cut the amberjack into small slices and the zucchini into strips. Boil the rice and drain it a few moments before the end of cooking. Fry the zucchini with 1 drizzle of oil in a non-stick casserole. After a few minutes add the amberjack, the rice and a little cooking water. Bring to cooking and finally add salt and pepper. Assembly. Place a pasta cutter in the centre of a plate and place the rice with the amberjack inside. Gently extract the coppapasta and season the timbale with 1 drizzle of oil emulsified with 1 teaspoon of soy sauce. Garnish with a light dusting of breadcrumbs and serve.

RICE, PUMPKIN AND GOOSE LIVER

Servings: 4 persons

Cooking Time   Cost   Difficulty

Ingredients:

- 300 gr diced pumpkin
- 280 gr rice
- 200g goose fat liver
- 80 gr butter
- 1 lt vegetable broth
- 2 shallots
- 60 gr grated parmesan cheese
- 16 goose liver nuts
- 20 boiled pumpkin nuts
- nutmeg
- cinnamon

Directions:

Cook a chopped shallot in a little butter, without browning; add the pumpkin cubes and season with a pinch of powdered cinnamon and nutmeg. Adjust the salt. Brown the other chopped shallot in butter in a saucepan and add the rice; toast it lightly and cook it for 7 minutes slowly adding the boiling stock. Continue with the cooked pumpkin and stir in the remaining butter and Parmesan cheese. Adjust the salt and let it rest covered for 3 minutes. Meanwhile, in a lightly greased non-stick pan, brown the liver and pumpkin cubes.

TORTELLONI WITH BERRIES

Servings: 2 persons

Cooking Time   Cost   Difficulty

Ingredients:

- 40 gr triple zero flour
- 2 gr black pepper
- 40 gr Fossa cheese
- 2 gr salt
- 20 gr grana cheese
- 50 gr speck
- 40 gr of semolina
- 20 gr whole eggs
- 20 gr mixed berries smoothies and sieved

Directions:

Prepare the filling by passing the speck through the meat grinder (two steps are necessary). Reduce the cheese into cream with the cutter by mixing it with the egg and grated parmesan cheese. Assemble by adding salt, pepper and speck. Put in vacuum in vacuum chamber machine 99 (maximum). To preserve and pasteurize, place the filling bag in a 62°C steam oven for 10 minutes. Then blast chill to +3°C. To make the pastry, knead the flours directly with the berries and eggs using a fresh dough kneading machine. Vacuum in a 99 vacuum bell machine (maximum) and leave to rest for at least 3 hours. Pass through the roller sheeter making 8 passes until you reach the desired dough height (0.2-0.3 mm are ideal: they must not be too thin to make the dough taste). With a round dough cutter with a diameter of 7 cm form circles of dough and fill them with the filling using a "sac à poche" (the proportion between filling and sheet must be 50% and 50%). Close the sheet creating a crescent and bring the two ends closer together to form tortellini. Moisten with egg yolk emulsion and water in equal parts, if necessary.

LINGUINE WITH TURBOT FISH, BUTTER, SAGE AND LIME

Servings: 4 persons

Cooking Time   Cost   Difficulty

Ingredients:

- 320 gr of linguine
- 2 garlic cloves
- 180 gr of turbot fillets
- 1 lime
- 40 gr of butter
- dehydrated raspberries
- 12 sage leaves
- salt

Directions:

To prepare the pasta with turbot, butter, sage and lime, cut out the fillets and keep them aside, in the meantime put a saucepan full of slightly salted water to boil.

Boil the turbot fillets for 15 minutes and keep them aside until they cool.

In the same pot as the fish, boil the pasta adding a little salt and bring it halfway through cooking.

In the meantime, the pasta cooks, chop and remove any bones from the fillet and keep it aside.

Melt the butter in a pan, then brown the poached garlic and sage, remove the garlic and transfer the pasta directly into the pan and bring it to cooking by adding cooking water whenever necessary.

One minute before the end of cooking, add the turbot and lime peel to the pan and stir in all the ingredients.

Season with a pinch of pepper and then add the dehydrated raspberries and more lime peel.

LASAGNE WITH SEAFOOD

Servings: 4 persons

Cooking Time   Cost   Difficulty

Ingredients:

- 1 Kg clams
- 250 g fresh pasta for very thin lasagne
- 8 scampi
- 200 g clean squid
- 1 white onion
- 1 Kg coppered tomatoes
- breadcrumbs
- 200 g fillets of sole
- Salt and pepper
- extra virgin olive oil

Directions:

Collect the clams in a bowl and cover them with water, to which you will have added a handful of salt. Let them purge for up to 12 hours in the refrigerator, changing the water from time to time. Then transfer them with your hands in a colander to make them drip, taking care not to move the impurities that will have deposited on the bottom of the bowl. Transfer the clams into a large saucepan, season them with 2 tablespoons of oil, cover them and leave them on the fire until they have opened (it will take about 5-6′). Turn off and shell them all except a dozen, from which you will remove only one shell valva. Filter the cooking liquid through a fine knitted strainer lined with absorbent cotton.

Cut the onion into slices and brown it in 2 tablespoons of oil for a couple of minutes, then salt, pepper, add the sliced coppered tomatoes and continue cooking over medium heat for 15′ (sauce). Brown the sole fillets for a couple of minutes on each side in a hot pan veiled with oil. Sprinkle them with salt, reduce them into chunks and keep them aside. Shell the langoustines and remove the black gut and reduce the squids to rings. Brown them both in a hot pan with a teaspoon of oil for 2-3′. Set them aside. Spread on the bottom of an oven dish a spoonful of sauce then lay down a first lasagna, cover with more sauce and stuff with some shelled clams, some squid rings, a few pieces of sole and a couple of scampi cut into pieces.

Continue in this order closing with a last lasagna (you will have to keep some fish aside to complete); sprinkle the lasagna with sauce, sprinkle with breadcrumbs and bake at 180 °C for 22-23′. Remove from the oven, complete with the fish set aside and the clams with the shell; bake for another 2′, bake and serve.

CANNELLONI WITH SHRIMPS AND ORANGES

Servings: 6 persons

Cooking Time   Cost   Difficulty

Ingredients:

- 1 Kg Red prawns
- 10 Yolks
- 200 g Fennel
- 2 Oranges
- Extra virgin olive oil
- 1 Egg
- 400 g Flour 00
- 50 g Sage
- 190 g Clean Spinach
- Salt and pepper

Directions:

Mix the flour with the yolks and egg, a pinch of salt and a teaspoon of oil. Let the dough rest for 30', covered. Shell the shrimps and cut them into very thin slices. Thinly slice also the slices of the oranges peeled alive. Mix the oranges with the shrimp and season with salt, pepper and a drizzle of oil. Blanch the sage leaves in boiling salted water with 2 spinach leaves. Cool them in water and ice, drain them and blend them with 40 g of oil, obtaining a pesto.

Roll the dough into very thin sheets, cut them into 18 squares of 9-10 cm side and dip them in boiling salted water for 1', cool them in cold water, drain them and place them on a cloth. Place a part of shrimp on each square and close it with a cannellone. Roast the spinach in a pan with a drizzle of oil and a pinch of salt, a few at a time, in one layer, so that they remain a little crispy.

Slice the fennel into very thin slices. Sprinkle the pasta with a little water and bake the cannelloni in the oven at 180°C for 2': the pasta heats up but the shrimp remains raw. Serve the freshly baked cannelloni on top of the spinach, complete with the fennel and season with sage pesto, a drizzle of oil and grated orange peel.

LASAGNE AND SMOKED SALMON PIE

Servings: 4 persons

Cooking Time   Cost   Difficulty

Ingredients:

- 200 g Fresh lasagna ready
- 200 g Robiola cheese
- 150 g Smoked salmon
- 100 g Milk
- 200 g Fresh cream
- Breadcrumbs
- 20 g Grated grain
- Butter
- Marjoram
- Pink pepper, salt and black pepper

Directions:

Mix the robiola with the cream and milk and season with salt, pepper and marjoram (robiola cream). Butter one baking dish or 4 small individual baking dishes and whip the pastry, alternating the lasagna with the robiola cream, pieces of salmon, a little breadcrumb and a little parmesan and chopped pink pepper.

Make at least 4 layers, complete with robiola cream and breadcrumbs in abundance. Bake at 200 °C in a ventilated oven for about 10 minutes; bake and leave to rest for a few moments before serving.

FISH RAVIOLI

Servings: 4 persons

Cooking Time   Cost   Difficulty

Ingredients for ravioli

- 200 gr of flour 00
- 2 eggs

Ingredients for the filling

- 1 seabass
- 1 cup of marsala liqueur
- 2 tablespoons of béchamel
- 1 garlic clove
- salt
- pepper

Seasoning Ingredients

- 400 gr of cherry tomatoes
- extra virgin olive oil
- 1 kg of mussels
- salt
- 1 clove of garlic

Directions:

Carefully clean the mussels and cook them in the pan for a few minutes.

Move them into a bowl, separate them from their water and shell them. Clean the sea bass and cut it into small chunks.

Cook it in a pan with the Marsala, garlic, salt, pepper and parsley. Then transfer everything to a mixer and blend.

Devote to the ravioli by combining the flour with the eggs.

Knead with your fingers until you get a brick, then let it rest for about 30 minutes.

Once you are back, roll out the dough with a sheeter. Add the béchamel sauce to the filling and fill the rectangles of dough at intervals. Overlay a second layer of pasta, cut to form the ravioli and seal the edges well.

Prepare the condiment by cooking the tomatoes, cut in half, with garlic, oil and salt. Then add the mussels and let them season for a few minutes. Cook the pasta in boiling salted water and, once raised, let it flavour in a pan for a few minutes.

Your fish ravioli are ready to be brought to the table.

PACCHERI WITH SWORDFISH RAGOUT

Servings: 4 persons

Cooking Time   Cost   Difficulty

Ingredients:

- 400 gr of swordfish
- 1 clove of garlic
- 300 gr of paccheri (pasta type)
- extra virgin olive oil
- 200 gr of cherry tomatoes
- salt
- 100 ml of tomato puree
- pepper
- 1/2 glass of dry white wine
- parsley

Directions:

After having washed and cut the tomatoes in half, remove the skin and the central bone of the swordfish and cut it into cubes.

In a large frying pan fry the garlic clove in the oil together with the parsley.

Add the swordfish cubes and cherry tomatoes and pour the wine letting it fade. Then put the puree and cook with a lid for about 10 minutes, turning from time to time. In the meantime, cook the paccheri in abundant salted water. Drain them al dente and fry them in a pan for just 1 minute. The paccheri with swordfish sauce are ready to be brought to the table.

TAGLIATELLE WITH SCAMPI AND PISTACCHIO PESTO

Servings: 4 persons

Cooking Time   Cost   Difficulty

Ingredients:

- 250 gr of tagliatelle
- 1 shot of brandy
- 400 gr of scampi
- 40 gr of chopped pistachios
- 1 carrot
- 20 gr of chopped almonds
- 1 celery stalk
- Parsley, oil and salt
- 1/2 onion
- 1 garlic clove

Directions:

Clean the scampi by removing the carapace and putting the heads aside.

Now prepare a bisque. In a large frying pan heat a drizzle of oil and add carrot, onion, celery in pieces and the heads of the scampi, blend with the brandy, then cover with boiling water and cook for 20 minutes.

Lift the langoustine heads and mash the vegetables, then filter everything and keep the resulting liquid aside. Prepare the pistachio pesto by putting the pistachios and chopped almonds, garlic, salt, pepper and oil in a bowl.

Blend everything until you get a cream. Brown a clove of garlic in a pan with the oil, add the scampi and after a minute the bisque. Cook the tagliatelle in plenty of salted water, drain and pour them into the pan with the sauce, then add the pistachio pesto. Blow it all in the pan for one minute. Then serve the tagliatelle with scampi and pistachios on plates.

PASTA WITH ALMONDS AND MUSSELS

Servings: 4 persons

Cooking Time

Cost

Difficulty

Ingredients:

- 320 gr of pasta
- 1 garlic clove
- 1.5 kg mussels
- 1 teaspoon of curry
- 40 gr of almonds
- parsley
- 50 gr of bread
- oil

Directions:

Clean the mussels by removing any incrustations and remove the beards then rinse them under running water.

Put the mussels in a pan with a lid and cook until the valves open. Shell the mussels (keep some mussels with the shell to decorate the plates) and filter the seafood liquid, keeping it aside. Soften the bread in a bowl with a ladle of mussel cooking water. In a large frying pan brown, a clove of garlic with oil and almonds.

Add the crumbled bread and curry.

Stir and let it flavour in the pan for a couple of minutes then blend everything adding oil and mussel cooking water until you get a thick cream.

Now add the shelled mussels.

In the meantime, cook the pasta in plenty of water in which you have added the remaining mussel liquid, then drain the pasta and pour it into the pan and add the chopped parsley.

Serve the Pasta with almonds and mussels garnishing the dishes with mussels with the shell kept aside.

SHRIMP AND ARTICHOKE RICE

Servings: 4 persons

Cooking Time   Cost   Difficulty

Ingredients:

- 300 gr of rice
- 1 litre of soup (1 carrot, 1 celery rib, 5 cherry tomatoes)
- 400 gr of artichoke hearts
- Butter
- 800 gr of shrimps
- Salt and pepper
- 2 shallots
- Parsley

Directions:

Clean the shrimp by removing their head, carapace and intestines.

Prepare a fish comic by simmering for half an hour in 1 litre of water the heads of the shrimps with some tomatoes, a celery rib and a carrot.

In a saucepan, brown the chopped shallot with a knob of butter. Cut the artichoke hearts into slices and add them to the shallot and let them season for a few minutes.

Now add the shelled shrimp tails.

Add the rice and toast it in the seasoning.

Blend with the white wine, turn up the heat to evaporate completely then add salt and pepper. Filter the comic strip and add one ladle at a time to the risotto, lower the heat and cook the shrimp and artichoke risotto adding, as it is absorbed during cooking, the comic strip (soup).

Once cooked the risotto, turn off the flame, add some butter and stir with a wooden spoon. Let the risotto with artichokes and shrimps rest for a couple of minutes, then serve it on plates with a sprinkling of parsley.

CUTTLEFISH BLACK RICE

Servings: 4 persons

Cooking Time   Cost   Difficulty

Ingredients:

- 300 gr of rice
- 70 ml of extra virgin olive oil
- 100 gr of shrimps
- white wine
- 500 gr of cuttlefish
- Pecorino cheese,
- salt and pepper
- 10 gr of cuttlefish black
- 1 tuft of parsley
- 1/2 shallot
- 1 lt of vegetable broth

Directions:

Clean the cuttlefish by starting to remove the bone.

Then remove the entrails, eyes and beak, then skin it.

Here you will find the complete guide. Finally, cut the cuttlefish into strips. Gently remove the bag of cuttlefish black, then put it in a bowl and make the black that you will need for the preparation of your risotto. In a large pan brown, the chopped shallot in 50 grams of oil.

Add the cuttlefish, let it flavour a few minutes and then add the shrimps. Cook for about 2 minutes over low heat stirring.

Then add the rice and let it toast for a couple of minutes, then blend it with the wine. Continue cooking the rice by adding one ladle of broth at a time.

Halfway through cooking add the squid ink.

When it will be a few minutes before the end of cooking add salt and pepper.

Turn off the flame and put some pecorino cheese and the remaining 20 grams of oil.

Add some fresh parsley at the end.

Your cuttlefish black risotto is ready to be brought to the table.

RICE WITH ZUCCHINI AND SALMON

Servings: 4 persons

Cooking Time   Cost   Difficulty

Ingredients:

- 200 gr of rice
- 600 ml of broth
- 250 gr of zucchini
- Salt and pepper
- 1 spring onion
- basil
- 30 gr of butter
- 100 gr of steamed salmon

Directions:

Clean the zucchini and grate them in a bowl.

Wilt the spring onion with the butter in a saucepan, then put the rice to toast.

Now add the zucchini and turn them over.

Cook the risotto adding one ladle at a time of hot broth.

When the cooking is almost finished put the chopped basil, salt, pepper and steamed salmon.

Stir gently.

Your rice with zucchini and salmon is ready to be brought to the table.

HOMEMADE TORTELLINI

Servings: 4 persons

Cooking Time   Cost   Difficulty

Ingredients:

- 200 gr of flour 00
- 1 egg
- 2 eggs
- 50 gr of grated parmesan cheese
- 100 gr of pork loin
- nutmeg
- 10 gr of butter
- Salt
- 100 gr of raw ham

Directions:

Cut the pork into pieces and remove the fatty parts.

Melt the butter in a non-stick pan then add the meat and brown it for a couple of minutes, then continue cooking over medium heat for about ten minutes.

Now put the meat, raw ham, Parmesan cheese, salt, pepper and nutmeg in a mixer.

Chop everything then adds the egg and mix well all the ingredients. In the meantime, prepare the pasta. Place the flour in a bowl or on a flat surface in a fountain with the eggs in the center. With the tips of your fingertips mix the flour with the eggs and let the flour gradually absorb from the edges. Knead for a long time until the dough is smooth and elastic.

Alternatively, you can use a kneading machine like I did.

Form a ball and let it rest for 15 minutes well covered.

Take the sheet of pasta and put it back on the pastry board and cut it into 2/3 pieces.

Flatten with a rolling pin one piece of dough at a time, then pass it in the dough machine putting the set roller in the widest thickness. Once passed, fold it in half and pass it again setting the roller in the thinnest thickness.

Place the sheets of dough obtained on a flat surface, interspersed with a little flour between one sheet and another.

Put the dough obtained in this way on the pastry board and cut it with a knife into squares of about 3 centimetres of side.

Put, in the center of each square, some filling.

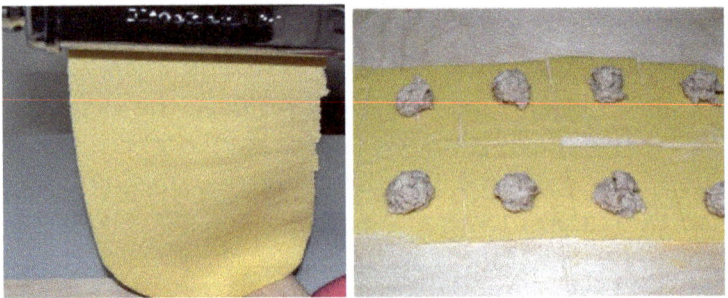

Wet your fingertips then close each square first in a triangle, then make a turn by rolling and finally seal by closing in a tortellino (the image is more explanatory). Prepare in this way all the tortellini that you will gradually put on a floured plate.

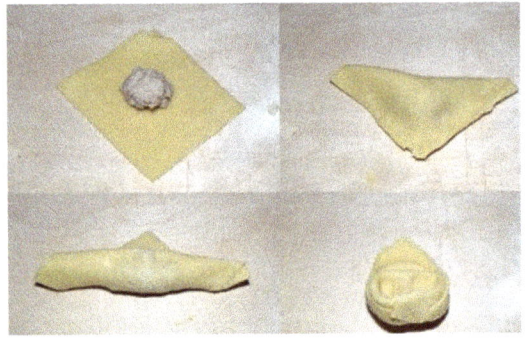

Then cook the tortellini in meat broth for about 15/18 minutes and serve with plenty of Parmesan cheese.

TORTELLINI IN THE OVEN

Servings: 6 persons

Cooking Time   Cost   Difficulty

Ingredients:

- 500 gr of tortellini pasta
- 50 gr of parmesan cheese
- 700 ml of tomato puree
- extra virgin olive oil
- 1 onion
- Salt
- 250 gr of mozzarella

Directions:

Chop the onion finely and fry it with a little oil in a saucepan.

Once browned, add the tomato puree and salt and stir. Cook the sauce over medium heat for at least an hour or until you get a nice, small sauce. In a pot with plenty of salted water cook the tortellini for half the time indicated on their packaging.

Lift them up and transfer part of them into a baking pan where you will have put a ladle of sauce. Then add the mozzarella cut into very small pieces and the grated Parmesan cheese. Now form the second layer putting again tortellini, sauce, mozzarella and parmesan cheese. Mix the ingredients by stirring gently. Cover everything with the remaining sauce, mozzarella and Parmesan cheese.

Cook the tortellini in a preheated oven at 180 °C for 20 minutes.

CANNELLONI RICOTTA AND SPINACH

Servings: 4 persons

Cooking Time   Cost   Difficulty

Ingredients:

- 250 g fresh lasagna sheets
- nutmeg
- parmesan cheese
- salt and pepper
- extra virgin olive oil
- 500 ml of milk
- 500 g spinach (fresh or thawed)
- 50 g of flour 00
- 450 g of ricotta cheese
- 50 g of butter
- 1/2 shallot

Directions:

Fry with a drizzle of oil half chopped shallot, after a few minutes add the spinach. We used the thawed ones, in this case a cooking time of about 10 minutes is enough; in case of fresh spinach it will be slightly longer. Let's add salt and pepper.

Once cooked, we transfer the spinach in a mixer and whisk them. Then we pour in a boule together with the ricotta cheese and add it to flavour the grated Parmesan cheese. Mix everything well, so as to obtain a nice creamy and homogeneous filling. Separately, we prepare the béchamel sauce. We boil the milk in a saucepan, while, apart, we melt the butter and, only when it is completely melted, we add the flour 00. Let it thicken, continuing to stir, for a couple of minutes, then we transfer this mixture into the milk, which has now reached boiling point. We flavour with nutmeg, stir then remove from the heat. Spread a little bit of it in a rectangular baking dish, then proceed to assemble the cannelloni.

We transfer the filling into a sac-a-poche and pour a strip on the short side of a fresh pastry sheet. We roll it up gently and put it in the baking dish. We proceed in this way until all the ingredients are exhausted.

Then we pour a layer of béchamel on the surface of the cannelloni, distributing it evenly.

We sprinkle a little grated Parmesan cheese and pour a drizzle of oil.

Then we cook in preheated oven at 180° for about 20 minutes.

After the necessary time, we take out and serve still hot our cannelloni ricotta and spinach.

PASTA WITH PUMPKIN FLOWER CREAM

Servings: 4 persons

Cooking Time   Cost   Difficulty

Ingredients for the cream:

- 150 gr of pumpkin or zucchini flowers
- 1 tablespoon of mixed for fried (chopped onion, celery and carrot)
- 40 gr of grated parmesan cheese
- salt
- 50 ml of fresh cream or milk
- extra virgin olive oil

Ingredients for pasta

- 300 gr of linguine or spaghetti
- 2 slices of bread without crust
- 5-6 anchovies

Directions:

First wash the pumpkin flowers and clean them (eliminating pistils and bases).

Then sauté them quickly in a pan with the mixture and a little oil, then blend them with the addition of cream (for a more delicate flavour, you can use milk or even water) and Parmesan cheese, then adjust the salt. Chop the anchovies and cut the bread into very small cubes, then fry them both in a pan with a little oil.

Keep them aside and instead transfer the cream of flowers in the same pan.

In the meantime, cook the pasta very al dente, drain it, then sauté it quickly in the pan with the flower cream, adding a little water to cook the pasta if needed.

The pasta with the cream of pumpkin flowers is ready: plate, complete with bread and anchovy crumble and serve immediately.

CONCHIGLIONI (SHELLS) STUFFED WITH PUMPKIN AND MOZZARELLA CHEESE

Servings: 4 persons

Cooking Time   Cost   Difficulty

Ingredients:

- 350 gr of shells
- 400 ml béchamel
- 600 gr of pumpkin
- 1 nut
- 250 gr of mozzarella
- Salt
- 100 gr of speck
- Pepper
- 30 gr of parmesan cheese
- Oil

Directions:

Clean the pumpkin and cut it into cubes, put it in a large frying pan with a drizzle of oil and let it flavour over a high flame for a couple of minutes. Add 1 vegetable cube, cover with half a glass of water and cook the pumpkin for about ten minutes. Turn up the heat and let the water dry completely, then add the bacon cut into strips, the cubes of mozzarella and 2/3 of Parmesan cheese.

Mix and season with salt and pepper. In the meantime, cook the conchiglioni in a pot with plenty of salted water. Drain the conchiglioni very al dente (my packet had 16 minutes of cooking time on it, I cooked them for 13 minutes) and, with the help of a teaspoon, start stuffing them with the pumpkin filling previously prepared. Place the conchiglioni in a baking dish covered with béchamel sauce.

Cover the conchiglioni with the béchamel sauce and the remaining Parmesan cheese, then bake at 180°C.

Cook for 20 minutes or until the surface is lightly gratinated.

Serve your conchiglioni filled with pumpkin and mozzarella in hot dishes.

RICE WITH PUMPKIN, GINGER AND TOASTED ALMONDS

Servings: 4 persons

Cooking Time   Cost   Difficulty

Ingredients:

- 900 ml of water
- Ginger
- 320 g of rice
- Gills almonds
- 50 ml of cream
- Pumpkin
- 50 g of Castelmagno cheese

Directions:

Let's cut the pumpkin into cubes and put it to cook in a pan, flavouring it with a little ginger. When it is cooked, whisk it in the mixer until it has a creamy consistency.

Let's dry toast the rice, and then add all at once, the salted water slightly heated in the microwave.

Let the rice cook over low heat, without stirring, until almost completely absorbed. Add the cream of pumpkin and salt and pepper.

Melt the Castelmagno in the microwave with the cream, filter with the strainer and pour over the risotto, garnishing with a few almond strips.

PROSECCO RICE

Servings: 4 persons

Cooking Time   Cost   Difficulty

Ingredients:

- 260 gr of rice
- 100 gr of sweet gorgonzola
- 1 spring onion
- Butter
- 300 ml of prosecco
- Salt
- 500 ml vegetable broth
- 40 gr of parmesan cheese

Directions:

Finely chop the spring onion and let it wither in a saucepan with butter.

Add the rice, stir it and let it toast for a couple of minutes.

Now put the prosecco, turn up the heat and let the alcoholic part evaporate.

Lower the heat and continue cooking adding one ladle at a time of hot broth. Add salt to taste. When cooked, stir in the gorgonzola.

At the moment of cooking, add crumbled parmesan wafers previously prepared.

To make them, just put a few tablespoons of Parmesan cheese in a drip pan covered with baking paper and cook them for a couple of minutes at 220 °C. Your risotto with prosecco is ready to be brought to the table.

RICE BALLS WITH PUMPKIN

Servings: 4 persons

Cooking Time   Cost   Difficulty

Ingredients:

- 250 gr of rice
- 1/2 cup of white wine
- 8 zucchini flowers
- 100 gr of scamorza cheese
- 250 gr of pumpkin already cleaned
- 1 knob of butter
- 1/2 onion
- 20 gr grated cheese
- 500 ml vegetable broth
- Salt and olive oil

Directions:

Cut the pumpkin into cubes, chop the onion and brown them both in a pan with a drizzle of oil. Add the rice and let it toast, then blend with the white wine. Cover everything with vegetable stock and start cooking, adding more stock, little by little, as it is absorbed. Butter some single-portion stencils and line them with zucchini flowers. Cook the rice very al dente, then add diced scamorza cheese, butter and grated cheese mixed together. Divide the risotto into moulds and bake at 180 °C in a preheated ventilated oven. Cook for about 20 minutes. Once out of the oven, let the timbales cool down for a few minutes, then turn them upside down on plates and serve.

APPLE RICE

Servings: 4 persons

Cooking Time   Cost   Difficulty

Ingredients:

- 2 green apples
- Salt
- 250 gr of rice
- Pepper
- 1 small onion
- 40 gr of grated provolone
- 40 gr of butter
- 500 ml vegetable broth
- Olive oil
- White wine

Directions:

Wash and clean the whole apple and cut it into cubes. Finely chop the onion and brown it in melted butter with a little oil, then add the apple.

Add the rice, stir and let it toast for a couple of minutes, until it becomes transparent, then add the white wine and let it fade.

At this point add salt, cover with the stock and start cooking, adding more stock one ladle at a time if necessary. At the end of cooking, season with salt and pepper and stir in butter and grated provolone. Finally, plate, decorate with slices of apple and serve the apple risotto.

RICE WITH SCAMPI CREAM

Servings: 4 persons

Cooking Time   Cost   Difficulty

Ingredients:

- 320 g of rice
- 2 litres of water
- 800 g of scampi (not too big)
- extra virgin olive oil
- 1 shot of brandy
- butter
- 1 shallot
- salt and pepper
- chopped parsley
- 50 ml of tomato puree
- 100 ml of cooking cream

Ingredients for soup:

- Celery
- 1/2 glass of dry white wine
- 1 shallot
- Salt
- 1-2 carrots
- 2-3 peppercorns
- 1 clove of garlic

Directions:

Let's start by preparing the soup that will be used to cook our risotto giving taste and flavour.

Wash all the scampi and proceed to eliminate heads and shells (the outer shells). Put aside the pulp, after eliminating the intestinal thread. Take a pot and fry a clove of garlic and a little oil with chopped shallot, carrots and celery. Add the heads (crushing them a bit), the carapaces and some pepper grains. Brown everything for a few minutes and then blend with the white wine. When it has evaporated, add the two litres of water and cook the soup over medium heat for at least 30 minutes. Once cooked, keep the stock warm.

For the scampi cream: brown the scampi with the oil and chopped shallot, add a pinch of salt and blend with the brandy. When the brandy has evaporated, add the tomato sauce (or tomatoes) and two ladles of soup. Cook it all for a few minutes, then blend it with the mixer, add a little chopped parsley and, if you want, some cooking cream.

Let's proceed with the preparation of the risotto.

Put some butter in the pot, let it melt and add the rice that you will toast well. Bring the rice to cook adding, little by little, the hot filtered soup.

Halfway through cooking add the scampi cream, a handful of salt and a pinch of pepper. While the risotto finishes cooking, place the 4 whole scampi left aside on a baking pan, season with a pinch of salt, a drizzle of oil and a handful of chopped parsley and cook in the oven at 180°-190° for 2-3 minutes. Before removing the pot from the heat, stir the risotto with a drizzle of extra virgin olive oil.

At this point you can serve: do not forget to garnish each dish with the whole langoustine, a little chopped parsley and a drizzle of oil.

ARTICHOKE CARBONARA

Servings: 4 persons

Cooking Time   Cost   Difficulty

Ingredients:

- 350 gr of linguine
- 3 eggs
- 400 gr of artichoke hearts
- 30 gr of pecorino cheese
- 80 gr of bacon
- Salt and pepper
- 1 clove of garlic
- Evo oil
- 200 ml of broth
- Parsley

Directions:

Cut the artichoke hearts into segments. Heat the oil in a large pan, add the bacon and garlic and brown for a few minutes. Add the artichokes, then the hot stock. Add salt and cook for about 15 minutes. In a bowl mix the eggs with salt, pepper and pecorino cheese: beat the ingredients until you have a creamy and well blended mixture. Cook the pasta in plenty of boiling salted water.

Drain al dente, pour into the pan with the artichokes, add the egg mixture. Stir to mix everything together.

Then serve the artichokes carbonara adding chopped parsley on the plates.

MARRIED SOUP

Servings: 6 persons

Cooking Time　　　　　Cost　　　　　Difficulty

Ingredients:

- 1 kg of endives
- 150 gr of ribs
- 300 gr of borage
- 1 carrot
- 700 gr of chicory
- 1 celery coast
- 1 kg whole hen
- 1 onion, salt and pecorino cheese
- 400 gr of beef armour
- 2 lt of water

Directions:

Clean celery, onion and carrot and cut everything into cubes.

Take the meat and clean the chicken from its innards. In a large pot put the chicken, the rib, the breastplate, celery, onion, carrot and salt. Cover with cold water and start cooking. When it reaches boiling point, calculate about 3 hours of cooking time. In the meantime, clean and clean the vegetables. Wash them well under running water then take them dripping with water and put them in a saucepan and blanch them. Once they are ready, drain and let them cool. When the broth is ready, lift the meat and degrease it (removing the film that forms on the surface) and strain it. Put the broth back into the pot and add the vegetables. Debone the chicken and cut all the meat into pieces before adding it to the vegetables, then add the cheese cubes. Cook for about 5 minutes more, just as long as the ingredients season each other. Serve your soup hot marinated adding some grated pecorino cheese to the dishes.

PASTA BEANS AND RICOTTA CHEESE

Servings: 4 persons

Cooking Time   Cost   Difficulty

Ingredients:

- 1 kg of fresh broad beans (about 300 gr)
- 30 gr of pecorino cheese
- 320 gr of pasta
- Oil
- 1/2 leek
- Salt
- 250 gr of ricotta cheese
- Pepper

Directions:

Slice the leek into thin slices, then put it in a large pan with oil and let it wither. Add the shelled broad beans, add salt and pepper and let it flavour for a minute. Then add a ladle of boiling water, cover with a lid and cook for about ten minutes. In the meantime, cook the pasta in plenty of salted water. Then put the ricotta, pecorino cheese and a ladle of water from the cooking of the pasta in a bowl and stir until a cream is obtained. Drain the pasta al dente, pour it into the pan with the broad beans, add the ricotta cream and sauté in the pan for 1 minute. Serve the pasta with the broad beans and ricotta, sprinkling the plates with a little pecorino cheese and a little pepper.

PASTA WITH PEPPERS

Servings: 2 persons

Cooking Time   Cost   Difficulty

Ingredients:

- 1 red bell pepper
- 60 gr of provola cheese
- extra virgin olive oil
- 2 cherry tomatoes
- 1/2 onion
- Basil
- 1 clove of garlic
- Salt
- 160 gr of half pens

Directions:

Wash the bell pepper and cut it into strips, now chop the onion.

Fry the onion and the whole clove of garlic in a pan with oil, then add the peppers. Cook for 20 minutes then put the tomatoes cut into cubes, salt and basil. Cook another 5 minutes stirring occasionally. In the meantime, cook the pasta in boiling salted water, drain it and sauté it in a pan. Your pasta with peppers is ready, serve it with julienne provola.

PUMPKIN CARBONARA

Servings: 4 persons

Cooking Time   Cost   Difficulty

Ingredients:

- 300 gr of pasta
- Sage
- 2 eggs
- Salt
- 600 gr of pumpkin
- Pepper
- 35 gr of pecorino cheese
- Extra virgin olive oil
- 1 clove of garlic
- 100 ml of broth

Directions:

In a large frying pan, brown the garlic in oil together with the sage.

After cutting the pumpkin into cubes, put it into the pan and sauté it for 10 minutes. Now add the hot stock and cook over high heat for another 10 minutes. Meanwhile put the eggs in a bowl with salt, pepper and pecorino cheese and beat them with a fork. Cook the pasta in plenty of boiling salted water and drain it al dente. Put it in a pan with a little cooking water and fry it for 1 minute. Turn off the flame, add the beaten eggs and mix quickly.

Your pumpkin carbonara is ready to be served.

PASTA WITH LENTIL RAGOUT

Servings: 4 persons

Cooking Time   Cost   Difficulty

Ingredients:

- 300 gr of pasta
- 400 gr of tomato puree
- 1/2 onion
- 500 ml of water
- 1 carrot
- Salt
- 1 celery coast
- Extra virgin olive oil
- 200 gr of lentils
- Thyme

Directions:

In a saucepan fry onion, carrot and celery all finely chopped.

Then put the tomato puree and cook for about 20 minutes.

Now add the dried lentils, water and thyme and cook for 1 hour.

At the end of cooking adjust the salt. Cook the pasta in plenty of boiling salted water, drain it and add it to the sauce. Serve the pasta with lentil sauce on the plates, adding, if you prefer, a sprinkling of pepper directly on the plates.

WALNUT LASAGNE

Servings: 6 persons

Cooking Time   Cost   Difficulty

Ingredients:

- 300 gr of lasagne
- 500 ml béchamel
- 200 gr of mozzarella
- 50 gr of grated parmesan cheese
- 150 gr of asiago cheese
- Salt
- 150 gr fontina cheese
- Oil

Ingredients nut sauce:

- 30 gr of butter
- 1 garlic clove
- 50 gr of parmesan cheese
- 2 tablespoons of extra virgin olive oil
- 100 gr of walnut kernels
- 2 tablespoons of water
- 1 tablespoon of pine nuts
- Salt and pepper

Directions:

Blanch the walnut kernels in boiling water for a few minutes. Chop the walnuts and pine nuts together.

In a large frying pan fry the garlic clove in butter, then lift it up and add the chopped walnuts and pine nuts. Add the Parmesan cheese, salt and pepper. Finally add 2 tablespoons of water and 2 tablespoons of oil, stir and set aside. In the meantime, prepare the béchamel sauce. Place the diced cheeses in a bowl.

Cook the lasagna sheets in a pot with salted water together with a tablespoon of oil. Lift the lasagna sheets al dente and place them gradually on a sheet.

Start now to assemble your walnut lasagna.

Cover the bottom of the pan with a veil of béchamel sauce and cover with a first layer of lasagna. Distribute a veil of béchamel sauce and walnut sauce.

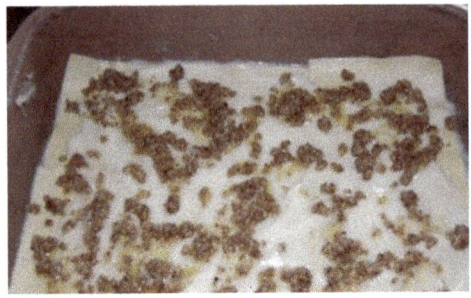

Then cover with the cheese and grated Parmesan cheese.

Cover with a layer of lasagna and continue alternating a layer of seasoning and a layer of lasagna until all the ingredients have been used up. Finish the preparation of the walnut lasagne with a layer of lasagne that you will cover with béchamel sauce, walnut sauce and Parmesan cheese.

Bake the walnut lasagne at 200° and cook for 30 minutes. Let your lasagne cool down before slicing and serving.

LEMON RICE

Servings: 4 persons

Cooking Time   Cost   Difficulty

Ingredients:

- 240 gr of rice
- 20 gr of butter
- 1 of organic lemon
- 25 gr of grain
- 1/2 of onion
- Olive oil
- 600 gr of broth
- Salt

Directions:

Chop the onion and let it wither in a saucepan with a drizzle of oil and butter. Meanwhile, wash the lemon and grate the peel very finely. Then squeeze the juice. Once the onion has withered, add the rice and toast it in the saucepan for a few minutes. When the rice starts to become transparent, add the boiling broth one ladle at a time. Halfway through cooking, add the lemon juice. Then, as the broth is absorbed, add more. Continue like this until the rice is cooked. Turn off the heat and add the lemon peel and grated Parmesan cheese. Add the lemon risotto and serve after a couple of minutes. Serve by decorating the plates with lemon heads.

CHAMPAGNE RICE

Servings: 4 persons

Cooking Time   Cost   Difficulty

Ingredients:

- 260 gr di riso
- 20 gr of parmesan cheese
- 1 scalogno
- 50 gr of provola
- 300 ml di champagne
- 1 knob of butter
- 500 ml di brodo vegetale
- Salt

Directions:

Prepare the vegetable stock.

Fry the peeled and veiled onion in a saucepan with butter. As soon as the onion is golden brown, add the rice, stir gently so that it toasts evenly. Wet the rice with half the champagne. When the champagne will be nuanced, complete the cooking of the risotto by adding the hot broth, one ladle at a time, alternating with the remaining champagne. Adjust the salt and always stirring, cook the rice pouring constantly on the broth, taking care not to let it dry. When cooked (about 20 minutes) remove the casserole from the heat, add the butter, Parmesan cheese and diced provola cheese and stir the risotto.

Wait a couple of minutes before serving the champagne risotto in the dishes, so that the rice rests and the flavors blend better.

LASAGNA ROLLS

Servings: 4 persons

Cooking Time   Cost   Difficulty

Ingredients:

- 250 gr of lasagne
- 500 ml béchamel
- 60 gr of dried porcini mushrooms
- 1 clove of garlic
- 150 gr of cooked ham
- Salt
- 150 gr of julienne cut cheese
- Oil

Directions:

Boil a saucepan with water, add salt and a tablespoon of oil and cook the lasagna sheets for a couple of minutes. Now lift the sheets and place them on a cloth to dry them.

Fry the porcini mushrooms, which you will have previously revived in warm water for 20 minutes, in a pan with a clove of garlic and a drizzle of oil. In the meantime, prepare the béchamel sauce.

Take one rectangle of pasta at a time, place it on aluminium foil and sprinkle it with a veil of béchamel sauce. Cover with the cooked ham, mushrooms and finally add the julienne cut cheese. Roll the dough on itself, until it forms a roll, wrap it in aluminium foil and proceed in the same way for all lasagna sheets. Place the rolls in the freezer to firm for about twenty minutes. Now take the rolls and cut them into slices 2/3 centimeters thick. Place the lasagna rolls in a baking tray in which you have spread a layer of béchamel sauce. Cover everything with the remaining béchamel and bake at 180°. Cook the lasagna rolls with ham and mushrooms for about 30 minutes, or until the surface of the béchamel sauce is just browned. Serve and enjoy your meal.

APPENDIX

Cooking Conversion Charts

Volume (liquid)	
US Customary	Metric
1/8 teaspoon	.6 ml
1/4 teaspoon	1.2 ml
1/2 teaspoon	2.5 ml
3/4 teaspoon	3.7 ml
1 teaspoon	5 ml
1 tablespoon	15 ml
2 tablespoon or 1 fluid ounce	30 ml
1/4 cup or 2 fluid ounces	59 ml
1/3 cup	79 ml
1/2 cup	118 ml
2/3 cup	158 ml
3/4 cup	177 ml
1 cup or 8 fluid ounces	237 ml
2 cups or 1 pint	473 ml
4 cups or 1 quart	946 ml
8 cups or 1/2 gallon	1.9 liters
1 gallon	3.8 liters

Weight (mass)	
US contemporary (ounces)	Metric (grams)
1/2 ounce	14 grams
1 ounce	28 grams
3 ounces	85 grams
3.53 ounces	100 grams
4 ounces	113 grams
8 ounces	227 grams
12 ounces	340 grams
16 ounces or 1 pound	454 grams

Oven Temperatures	
US contemporary	Metric
250° F	121° C
300° F	149° C
350° F	177° C
400° F	204° C
450° F	232° C

Volume Equivalents (liquid)		
3 teaspoons	1 tablespoon	0.5 fluid ounce
2 tablespoons	1/8 cup	1 fluid ounce
4 tablespoons	1/4 cup	2 fluid ounces
5 1/3 tablespoons	1/3 cup	2.7 fluid ounces
8 tablespoons	1/2 cup	4 fluid ounces
12 tablespoons	3/4 cup	6 fluid ounces
16 tablespoons	1 cup	8 fluid ounces
2 cups	1 pint	16 fluid ounces
2 pints	1 quart	32 fluid ounces
4 quarts	1 gallon	128 fluid ounces

Lightning Source UK Ltd.
Milton Keynes UK
UKHW021914190221
378991UK00005B/55

9 781801 820844